Wild Boars AND Teacup Pigs

HENRY THATCHER

PowerKiDS press.

New York

Published in 2014 by The Rosen Publishing Group, Inc.
29 East 21st Street, New York, NY 10010

First Edition

Produced for Rosen by Cyan Candy, LLC
Editor: Joshua Shadowens
Designer: Erica Clendening, Cyan Candy

Photo Credits: Cover (top), pp. 4, 6, 8, 9, 10–11, 12, 13, 14, 15, 16, 18, 19 , 20, 21, 26, 27, Shutterstock.com; cover (bottom), p. 24 courtesy Orbora78/Flickr; p. 5 itchydogimages on Flickr; pp. 7, 29 maveric2003/Flickr; pp. 17, 28 © 2012–2013, David R. Schroeter. All rights reserved; pp. 22–23 © June Hopper Hymas/Flickr; p. 25 © Harumi Akabane/Flickr; p. 30 Wikimedia Commons; p. 31 Mark Peters, via Wikimedia Commons.

Library of Congress Cataloging-in-Publication Data

Thatcher, Henry.
 Wild boars and teacup pigs / by Henry Thatcher. — First edition.
    pages cm. — (Big animals, small animals)
 Includes index.
 ISBN 978-1-4777-6097-0 (library) — ISBN 978-1-4777-6098-7 (pbk.) —
 ISBN 978-1-4777-6099-4 (6-pack)
 1. Swine—Juvenile literature. 2. Wild boar—Juvenile literature. I. Title.
 SF395.5.T43 2014
 636.4—dc23

                              2013028105

Manufactured in the United States of America

CPSIA Compliance Information: Batch #W14PK2: For Further Information contact Rosen Publishing, New York, New York at 1-800-237-9932

Table of Contents

Two Pigs, Big AND Small

What do you think of when you picture a pig? Do you think of a large pink animal laying around in a mud puddle? Pigs are part of the *Sus* family. There are ten living species of pig, including wild boars. The **domesticated** pig is actually a subspecies of the wild boar. This means domesticated pigs' ancestors were wild boars, and they still share some of the same qualities.

Here, a young teacup pig relaxes on its owners' couch.

Wild boars are large pigs, though their size varies depending on the kind of boar. All wild boars have big heads with flat snouts, round bodies, and short legs. On the other side of the size scale are a kind of domesticated pig called the teacup pig. As the name suggests these pigs are bred to be small. Let's find out more about the wild boar and its small cousin, the teacup pig.

Here, a giant wild boar takes a rest in some mud.

Where IN THE World?

Wild boars are **native** to many places around the world. This includes northern and central Europe, the Mediterranean, and Asia, including Russia, Japan, India, and Indonesia. They have been introduced to North America and South America, the Caribbean islands, parts of Africa, and Australia and the surrounding islands. In the United States, wild boars are found only in the southern states, such as Florida, Georgia, Louisiana, and parts of Texas and California. Some of these places have relatively large **populations** of boar.

This is a fully grown miniature pig. As you can see, they can grow to be quite large, don't let the name fool you.

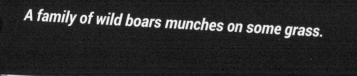

A family of wild boars munches on some grass.

Teacup pigs live all around the world, wherever people want to keep them. You see, unlike wild boars, they are domesticated. This means that people keep them for pets.

Home Sweet Home

Wild boars are very **adaptable**. This means they are able to change to fit new environments, climates, and food sources. They live in forests, grasslands, coastal areas, foothills of mountains, and pretty much anywhere there is enough water and food to be found. Wild boars do not prefer dry, desert **habitats**, or to live high up in the mountains. They can live in warm,

Three very young wild boars look for something to eat in the snow.

tropical places or in cold, harsh places like Siberia, in Russia. Though they can live in many different habitats, they tend to like places that have dense vegetation, such as forests. Wild boars are mostly **nocturnal**, which means they come out at night to look for food.

 Two male wild boars challenge each other for space near a pond.

In many cases, wild boars have been introduced into areas where they would not normally live by people. This is usually done so people can hunt the boars. However, in some of these areas, the boars have become invasive species. This means they are doing so well in the new habitat that they are hurting plants and animals that originally lived there.

A group, also called a drove, of young wild boars run along.

BIG FACT!

The first person to breed teacup pigs was Chris Murray, from England. There were many other kinds of mini pigs bred before his, but none were given the name "teacup" pigs.

Are They Alike?

Teacup pigs and wild boars seem pretty different, don't they? One is a cute pet, while the other is a large, tusked, wild pig. However, both animals are pigs and therefore have many similarities, aside from their size.

This is a fully-mature, 15-year-old male wild boar.

Here is a typical American female pig, also known as a sow, with one of her piglets.

PIGLET

Pigs have large heads with a flat snout at the end. This snout is used to root, or dig, in the soil to find food. A pig's snout is excellent at sniffing out yummy underground treats! This is a good thing, because pigs do not have very keen eyesight.

Pigs have four toes on each foot. The two center toes are bigger and take most of the weight as the pig walks.

Male pigs grow tusks. These tusk are the upper and lower canine teeth, which are growing all the time. The tusks become sharp as the upper and lower teeth rub against each other. The males use the tusk as a defense but also as tools for digging and looking for food. Male pigs are called boars or hogs. Female pigs are called sows, and do not grow tusks.

BIG FACT!

Wild boars are fast. They can run at speeds up to 30 miles per hour (48 km/h). They are good swimmers, too.

Pigs are covered in bristly hairs that are sometimes used by people to make brushes. They are hunted in the wild or domesticated for their meat. Bacon, ham, and pork are all examples of pig meat. Pigs provide nearly 40 percent of all the meat people eat worldwide.

YOUNG WILD BOAR

Comparing WILD BOARS

Size (length)...... Between 22 and 40 inches (55–100 cm) at the shoulder

Habitat.............. forests with dense plant life; can adapt to many habitats

Diet.................. omnivore, mainly plants, roots, mushrooms, or anything it can find

Predators .... humans, big cats, wolves, and birds of prey

Prey.................. birds, eggs, earthworms, and insects

Life Span........... 15 to 20 years

AND TEACUP PIGS

Size (length) ..... up to 16 inches (40 cm) at the shoulder

Habitat .... domesticated; lives with people

Diet .... omnivore, mainly vegetables, teacup pig food, and hay

Predators .... big cats, wolves, and coyotes

Prey .... insects, worms, and other small animals they may find while foraging

Life Span .... 15 to 20 years

One Big Pig!

Wild boars are large **mammals**. They can grow to be 3 feet (1 m) tall and 380 pounds (175 kg). Most are smaller than that, though. The average size for a male boar is around 200 pounds (90 kg). Females are not as big as the males.

Here, two adult male wild boars fight. Adult males are solitary, except to mate, so run-ins between males can be dangerous.

Male wild boars tend to be **solitary**. They look for a **mate** twice a year. They will fight other males for the right to mate with a female. Females give birth to one to two litters per year, with 4 to 10 piglets in each litter. They give birth in a nest they build from leaves, grasses, and moss. The nests are usually within very dense plants, so they are hard to find.

 A giant wild boar is in the forest hunting for food.

Once the babies are born, the females live together with other females and their young. These groups are called sounders and can have between 6 and 30 boars in them. The baby boars have different coat colors than do adult boars, which are usually brown, gray, or reddish-brown. Babies are born with light brown fur with cream and brown stripes running down their sides. Babies stay in the nest for the first two months and become independent at around 7 months. Wild boars can live between 15 to 20 years.

Three juvenile wild boars are out in the grass looking for a snack. ▶

Here is an adult female wild boar with her farrow, or litter, of piglets.

BIG FACT!

Wild boar tusks can grow to be a 2.5 inches (6 cm) long. That may not sound like much, but tigers have been found with holes from being gored by boar tusks.

Tiny as a Teacup

Teacup pigs start life as tiny as a teacup, just as their name suggests. This breed of domesticated pig is also called a micro pig, micro mini, mini pig, among other names. No matter what they are called, they are bred using potbellied pigs that have been selected over time for their small size. Potbellied pigs are a pig native to Vietnam. They are naturally much smaller than European or American livestock pigs. They tend to be around the size of a medium or

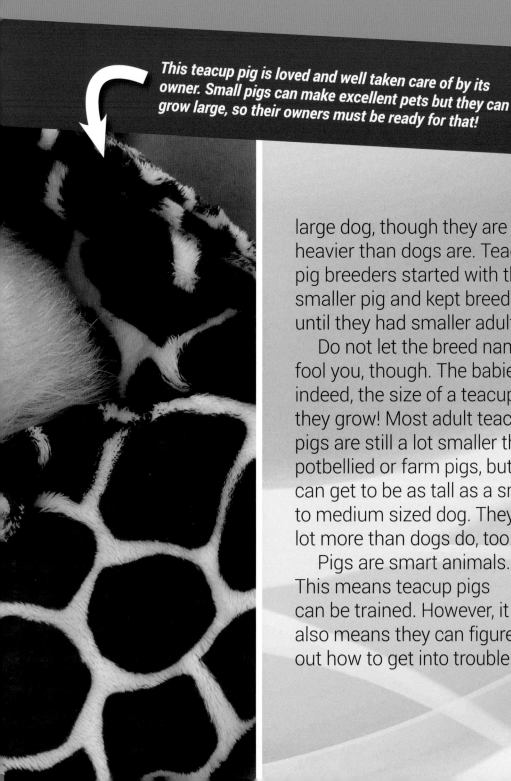

large dog, though they are much heavier than dogs are. Teacup pig breeders started with this smaller pig and kept breeding until they had smaller adults.

Do not let the breed name fool you, though. The babies are, indeed, the size of a teacup, but they grow! Most adult teacup pigs are still a lot smaller than potbellied or farm pigs, but they can get to be as tall as a small to medium sized dog. They eat a lot more than dogs do, too.

Pigs are smart animals. This means teacup pigs can be trained. However, it also means they can figure out how to get into trouble.

Pigs have been known to figure out how to open up food pantries and refrigerators.

Teacup pigs can sleep inside or outside. They would most like a place to spend at least some of their time

Miniature pigs can be trained to use a litter box, just as a cat would. Unfortunately, sometimes they also lay in it!

BIG FACT!

People who want to own teacup pigs should do their research and check out the size of the breeding adults. Sometimes teacup pigs have been known to grow into 350 pound (160 kg) pigs!

outdoors, where they can use their natural **instincts** to look for food. If they are outdoor pets, they need a shelter and warm bedding to keep them warm year-round. All pets need proper food, water, and medical care.

Diets: Big AND Small

Pigs are omnivores. This means they will eat almost anything, including plants, animals, and insects. Wild boars eat whatever is available in their habitat or depending on the season. For example, their diet in the spring might be made up of grasses, **forbs**, roots, and **tubers**. In the summer and fall they might eat grapes, plums,

Here, an adult and juvenile boar eat on a feeding ground on a farm.

prickly pears, mesquite, acorns, and persimmons, depending on where they live. Boars will also eat mushrooms, carrion, and even birds, eggs, snails, insects, earthworms, and other invertebrates. Wild boars can also be pests to farmers, as they are more than happy to make a meal out of agricultural crops.

Teacup pigs are omnivores, too. If they lived in the wild, they would eat much of the same types of food as the wild boar, only in smaller amounts.

27

However, as they are often kept as pets, they should be fed a balanced diet that meets all their nutritional needs. They need to be fed a lot of vegetables each day. They can be fed grains and specially-made teacup pig food that has the right amounts of proteins, fats, vitamins, and minerals the teacup pig needs to stay healthy. Teacup pigs can be given fruit twice a day as a treat, but owners need to be careful

Here, a miniature pig, also known as a potbellied pig, eats cereal off of the sidewalk. Pigs will eat almost anything.

BIG FACT!

Pigs also do not have a part of the brain that tells them they are full, a teacup owner must leave out only the right amount of food. If the pig is given too much food, it will eat all day!

not to overdo it. Teacup pigs will happily forage in your yard or garden, or even in your kitchen cabinets, so pig owners need to pig proof places where they do not want their pigs to go.

Big or Small, Does It Matter?

Wild boars and teacup pigs are both part of the same family. Wild boars **evolved** over thousands of years to take their current form. Humans started domesticating pigs some 9,000 years ago for their meat and hides, and in the past century people started breeding teacup pigs to become companion animals. Pigs sure have come a long way.

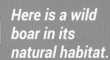
Here is a wild boar in its natural habitat.

Here, a group of Yorkshire pigs wallow in the mud at a pig sanctuary, which is a place pigs are brought to be safe. All types of pigs have lots of things in common, liking the mud is one of them!

Because these animals are adaptable, they have thrived in many habitats in the wild and on farms. The biggest danger for wild pigs is from habitat loss. As people start to recognize the importance of making rooms for all Earth's creatures, this loss of habitat may start to slow. Lets hope it does, so that there will always be room for both wild boars and teacup pigs to live and do well.

BIG FACT!

The Wild boar's two main predators are tigers and wolves. In India, tigers are known to follow boar sounders and eat the animals one by one. In Siberia, one wolf pack may eat up to 80 boars each year.

31

Glossary

adaptable (uh-DAPT-uh-bul) Able to change to fit new requirements.

domesticated (duh-MES-tih-kayt-id) Raised to live with people.

evolved (ih-VOLVD) Changed over many years.

forbs (FORBZ) Small plants with broad leaves.

habitats (HA-buh-tats) The surroundings where an animal or a plant naturally lives.

instincts (IN-stinkts) Feelings creatures have that help them know what to do.

mammals (MA-mulz) Warm-blooded animals that have backbones and hair, breathe air, and feed milk to their young.

mate (MAYT) A partner for making babies.

nocturnal (nok-TUR-nul) Active during the night.

populations (pop-yoo-LAY-shunz) Groups of animals or people living in the same area.

solitary (SAH-leh-ter-ee) Liking to be alone.

tropical (TRAH-puh-kul) Having to do with the warm parts of Earth that are near the equator.

tubers (TOO-berz) Nutrient-rich plant structures, often in the roots, as sweet potatoes, or in the stems as with potatoes.

Index

Websites

Due to the changing nature of Internet links, PowerKids Press has developed an online list of websites related to the subject of this book. This site is updated regularly. Please use this link to access the list: www.powerkids.com/basa/pig/